21 Quick Ways to Get More Clients

2nd Edition 2014

Non-Introduction

A normal author would include an introduction here, to tell you how wonderful he is and how much these 21 proven marketing tips can build your business ...

However. I am not normal. And time is short. You don't have time for small talk. What you need is to sell more good things to more clients, more often.

So let's get to it. Here are ...

21 Quick Ways to Get More Clients ...

so you can quit work early this Friday ☺

First, the table of contents, to prioritize your reading ...

Table of Contents

1) The Quickest Way to Get More Sales (the Girl Scout Cookie Phenomenon Explained)

Three Girl Scouts want to sell me some cookies. But I can buy from only one. Who will get my money?

Girl Scout #1 asks, "Hey, mister! Wanna buy some cookies?"

Girl Scout #2 asks, "Hey, mister Donlin! Wanna buy some cookies?"

Girl Scout #3 asks, "Hey, Daddy! Wanna buy some cookies?"

The answer, of course, is Girl Scout #3.

Why?

Because I know her, I trust her, and I want her to succeed.

Because the easiest person to sell to is someone who knows you, trusts you, and wants you to do well.

That's why all Girl Scouts selling cookies (or any kid selling anything), always start with their own family, then hit the next-door neighbors, before venturing out to sell to strangers.

In your business, you probably can't earn a living selling to your family and neighbors ...

But you can earn a very good living selling to people who know you, trust you, and want you to do well.

Who are these incredibly valuable people?

Your current clients.

They know you (if you keep in touch with them), they trust you (if you're not incompetent or a crook), and they want you to do well (so you can stay in business and keep making their life better).

When you have happy clients, you have a receptive audience to everything you may want to sell in the future.

Finding new and better ways to serve your clients, so they will favor you with repeat and referral sales, may not be as easy as selling cookies to your dad.

But it beats the heck out of cold calling or prospecting, which we all dread anyway. Why put yourself through it?

So ... the quickest way to get more sales is to sell more things to your current clients.

Notes:

2) "Force" Google to Help Write Your Next Ad

This one is sneaky. But like all the tips you'll discover in this book, it's 100% legal – and fun. Because why be in business if you can't have fun?

Now. Look at this screen capture of Google search results ...

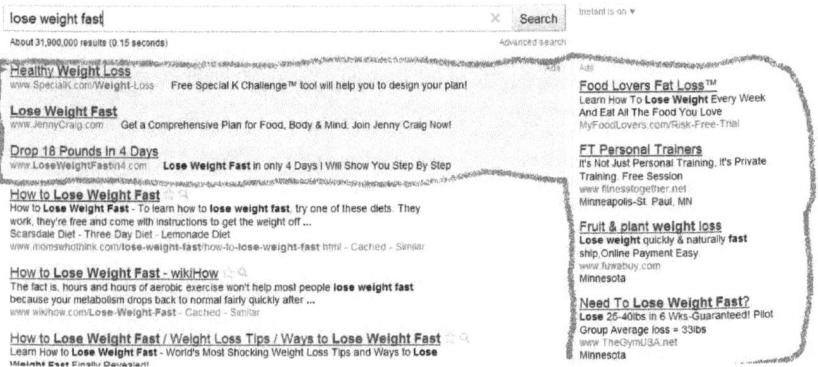

See those listings circled in red?

Those are Google AdWords, which people wrote and paid Google to display every time somebody searched for the terms "lose weight fast." The AdWords you see first are usually the ads that people have bid the most money to display.

In a highly competitive market like weight loss, advertisers may pay Google from $4 to $10 – or more – per click, just to get on page one of the search results. So you usually see some very good ads written by very smart and successful people.

Before writing any sales letter, web page, or print ad for your business, you should search Google for terms related to what your business sells.

That way, you can snoop on what competitors are saying in their ads and get ideas for your own ads – ideas you never would have thought of on your own. (Just don't steal anything word-for-word.)

But you probably knew that.

Okay. What's *new* about this "force Google to help create my ad" technique? This -- look at the next screen capture …

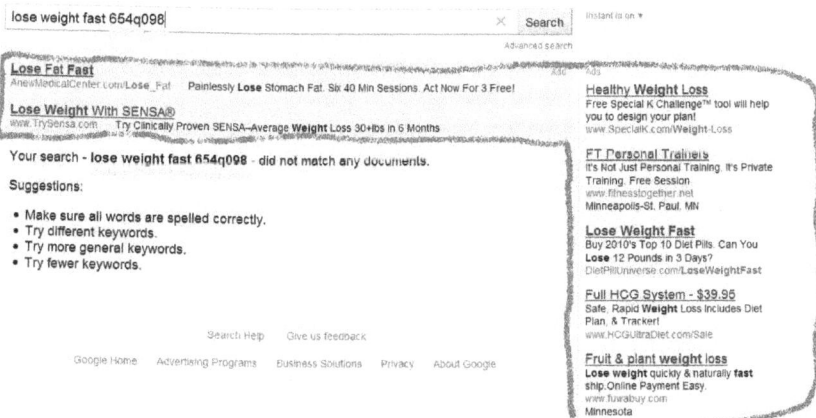

It's just like the last search, but with one BIG difference.

See that garbage underlined in yellow? The meaningless *654q098*?

When you search for garbage along with a valid phrase, like "lose weight fast," you confuse Google. You force it to show you the BEST-PERFORMING ads related to your search.

Because Google wants to make the most money at <u>all</u> times, you will see ads that Google has found get the most clicks on terms directly and *indirectly* related to your "garbage" search.

Take a look at the ads in the second example and you will see the very best ideas Google can find to help guide your own ad-writing efforts.

Examples:

- While you may think "lose weight fast," the first ad in the "Google garbage" results has the headline: **Lose Fat Fast**. Maybe that's a more profitable angle for your ads?
- The second ad in the "Google garbage" results has the headline: **Lose Weight With SENSA®**. Ever heard of this competitor? They're paying a LOT for clicks on Google. Maybe you should check out their marketing?
- Etc. etc. etc.

Use the "Google garbage" method to get new, creative ideas. Then use these ideas to write ads that sell more.

Notes:

3) How to Spy on Your Prospects for Fun (and Money)

Why spy your prospects? To uncover their "hot buttons," of course.

Definition: A hot button is an emotional reason that causes people to buy what you're selling. Think of it as the itch they want to scratch ... or the craving they want to fulfill.

In golf, for example, men may *say* they want to shave 5 strokes off their game, or hit more fairways in regulation. But if you try to sell golf clubs or lessons that appeal to those motives, you likely won't meet with huge success.

Why?

Because the hot button for most male golfers is this: They want to slam their tee shots 350 yards straight down the fairway, causing their buddies to turn 9 shades of green with envy.

Is this rational or logical? No. (And neither is golf, by the way). But it is reality.

That's why you see so many ads for golf clubs that claim to deliver more yards off the tee. The advertisers of "Big Betsy" type drivers are almost comical in the way they try to outdo each other's claims for distance ... yet, they sell. Like hotcakes.

Now. Back to your prospect.

You can't depend on prospects to tell you their hot buttons. And why should they? When you find them, you can push them– and cause your prospects to open their wallets, almost unconsciously.

So hot buttons are important. But finding them can be tricky.

Would you like to know how to uncover them? Without your prospects' knowledge or cooperation?

First, promise that you're selling a service or product that is 100% legal and ethical. Because I can't let this information fall into the wrong hands. Promise? Pinky swear?

Okay. Here's the easiest way to spy on your prospects and uncover hot buttons ...

Read their email.

No, no -- not like that.

This is easier than hacking into a Gmail account. Also legal.

First, look at this opening of a very successful sales letter I wrote several years ago ...

Don't you hate it?

- You apply online for jobs you KNOW you're perfect for -- and nothing happens ...
- You hand your resume to friends -- and they ALL have different ideas to improve it ...
- You revise your resume over and OVER -- and you still don't have a job ...

You're not going crazy.

And you're not alone ...

Today's job market is a living nightmare.

Want proof? The average time to find a job is now 33.6 weeks -- more than 8 MONTHS -- according to Sept. 2010 data from the U.S. Bureau of Labor Statistics.

See those three bullet points?

Each addresses a different problem my readers want fixed. These are hot buttons.

Every prospect reading this sales letter has one or more of those problems. When they see their problem in the first 3 lines of the letter, they nod their head in agreement. They think I am talking to them, because I *am* talking to them! I have pushed a hot button – I have reminded them of an itch they want to scratch.

How did I find these hot buttons? By reading emails my prospects had sent me in the months before I wrote that sales letter.

Yes, it took a few hours of research to read, organize, collate, and prioritize the problems people wrote about in their emails. But after I did the research, I had a nice list of hot buttons -- written by my prospects *in their own words*. Powerful.

You can do this, too.

Start saving and organizing every email you get from prospects and clients. Search through them for questions about your service or product ... requests for help ... complaints ... problems, etc.

Emails from prospects and clients are full of gold nuggets, in the form of hot buttons. They are your market talking to you.

Push the hot buttons you find in your email in-box and you can improve every sales letter, web page, or print ad you write.

Notes:

4) Another Way to Spy on Your Prospects

This one is even sneakier ...

You see, every prospect for every service or product probably reads at least one blog. And every blog has something you should know about, something that can uncover just as many hot buttons as reading your prospects' email.

That something is **the comments section**.

Forget the blog postings themselves. The comments your prospects leave on blogs are a *goldmine* of information, providing plenty of hot buttons for you to push in the marketing materials you write.

Here's an example, below. This blog, "Six Minutes," is devoted to helping readers become better public speakers ...

(Used by kind permission of http://sixminutes.dlugan.com)

And here's a screen capture showing some of the many reader comments on this blog. Do you see any potential hot buttons?

16 Comments

Lisa Braithwaite — Apr 21st, 2008

Great point, Andrew. I used to think there was something "wrong" with the way I prepared for a talk, because I didn't use all the breathing, relaxation and visualization techniques that were recommended.

Then I learned that there are two kinds of pre-performance rituals: one where you actively focus on the event by visualizing yourself speaking, etc., and one where you disassociate yourself from the event, as in distracting yourself with music, talking to the audience, and other activities that are not related to your speech (or race, or performance).

Whew! Now I enjoy my preparation rituals and don't feel guilty about them.

Lee Potts — Apr 21st, 2008

I can't agree strongly enough with Activity #1. Many, many of the problems that I've seen during presentations could be traced back to the speaker showing up at the last minute and assuming that everything will work perfectly and that nothing will need adjustments.

If a speaker arrives early, there's time to recover from the kind of problems that happen before your talk even begins: computer not booting, dead projector bulb, missing flip chart, etc.

Andrew Dlugan — Apr 21st, 2008

Lisa:
Good point, Lisa. While I like to stretch out my body (my neck in particular) before speaking, I have not adopted the strict relaxation and visualization techniques you refer to. Yet, I know some great speakers who swear by those techniques. It's a very

(Used by kind permission of http://sixminutes.dlugan.com)

If I were marketing to speakers, I might say,

> *Has this ever happened to you? You've visualized your speech. Practiced every word. You're ready*

*to go. But you arrive at the seminar location and --
disaster! Your computer won't boot up. And the
event planner thought YOU would bring a flip
chart. You're scheduled to go on in 30 minutes –
and you have no visuals. What do you do?*

That's a made-up example that took me less than 2
minutes to write. I just picked one set of hot buttons –
missing or malfunctioning equipment – from one set of
blog comments to create a powerful opening to a sales
letter.

**When you read the comments on the blogs your
prospects read, they will tell you -- in their own
words -- what's really bothering them.**

**As a result, you can sell more. Because you can
push their hot buttons while using their own
words to sell them.**

Notes:

5) One More Way to Spy on Your Prospects

This is my favorite: **Read book reviews on Amazon.**

Just like blogs, most of your prospects read books. Many book readers also post reviews on Amazon. And reviews are another rich source of hot buttons for you to exploit.

Here's an example review, for the book *Guerrilla Marketing for Job Hunters 2.0*:

43 of 43 people found the following review helpful:

★★★★★ **A Swiss Army Knife for the Job Seeker.** Don't leave home without it !!, March 3, 2010

By Brian Reiden (Ottawa, Ontario Canada) - See all my reviews

This review is from: **Guerrilla Marketing for Job Hunters 2.0: 1,001 Unconventional Tips, Tricks and Tactics for Landing Your Dream Job (Paperback)**

I actually had sought out this book (which was reserved and couldn't be taken out of the library) after seeing David Perry speak at a job search group meeting. When I starting leafing through the book, I realized that there was too much information in this book for me to keep coming into the library to copy down a page or two for something to try in my job search. I needed a copy right by the computer to use to try some of the tools that I would read about. Although I was on LinkedIn and thought I was using many of the tools available, I found I was quite wrong. I found this book to be very inspirational in its approach, what I needed to get my act together and how to organize a proper job search strategy. There is advice, in the form of scripts, for many different situations when making contacts with potential employers. It is a metaphorical Swiss-Army knife for the job seeker, something that you should not be without.

Help other customers find the most helpful reviews   Report abuse | Permalink

Was this review helpful to you? (Yes) (No)   Comment (1)

See that parts circled in red?

"A Swiss Army Knife for the Job Seeker" is a potentially brilliant headline for an ad, one I never would have thought of. What ideas are *your* prospects posting in their Amazon reviews?

And the underlined sentence about LinkedIn is a bit hot button. It could easily be turned into a bullet point for a sales letter, like this:

- Are you on LinkedIn? You may *think* you're using all the tools available, but are you? If recruiters and headhunters aren't calling, you're probably making this simple mistake (see page 87).

Get the idea? You can make your cash register ring like a Salvation Army bell when you find and push the right hot buttons.

But you'll never know what those hot buttons are until you start researching what your prospects say and think. And reading their book reviews on Amazon is an easy way to do it.

Best part: Those hot buttons are out there, right now, waiting for you to find them -- at no charge. You or any competent copywriter can do it.

Notes:

6) Improve Your Marketing, in 30 Seconds, with the Painless "Colonoscopy" Technique

Did you know that providing your service or products to clients is exactly like a colostomy? Let me explain ...

At a recent seminar, marketing master Seth Godin said something profound, which I wrote down (lucky you!). He said: "People judge their entire colonoscopy experience based on what they remember from the last 30 seconds."

Is that rational? Logical? No, and no. But, just like those irrational male golfers a few pages ago, this is reality.

In other words, last impressions make *lasting* impressions. And here's what that means for your business ...

The last time I took my car for a tune-up to one particular auto shop, he did a good job that was fairly priced. But I never went back. Why?

Because he spilled a full bottle of STP gas treatment on the front seat, cleaned it up poorly, then apologized half-heartedly -- and only after I confronted him about it. That's the part of the experience I remembered.

Take a long look at the last "30 seconds" of whatever you do for your clients. Are you leaving the best lasting impression? If not, fix it. If you don't, your clients' last contact with you may be their ... last contact with you.

7) The Secret of "Atomic" Marketing (From the Man Who Inspired Albert Einstein)

Remember high school geometry?

You may have hated it, like me, but you have to admit -- those theorems were elegant.

And not much had changed in geometry in the 2,300+ years since Euclid first drew triangles in the sand with a stick.

For example, nothing seemed more eternal than the fact that two parallel lines can never meet. Like train tracks, two lines running side by side will never touch each other, right?

Wrong.

In *Further Along The Road Less Traveled*, author and physician M. Scott Peck writes:

> ... Bernhard Riemann was a German mathematician who, back in the middle of the nineteenth century, asked himself, "What if two parallel lines do meet?" And on the assumption that two parallel lines do meet, and a couple of other alterations he made to Euclid's theorems, he developed a totally different geometry. [And] much of Albert Einstein's work, including that which led to the development of the atomic bomb (via the theory of relativity) ... was based not on Euclidean geometry but on Riemannian geometry.

The discovery of atomic power and other breakthroughs happened because one obscure math maven questioned one "fact" that all the experts took for granted.

So ... what does geometry have to do with marketing your business? Everything.

Because marketing is full of "facts" that everyone takes for granted.

But what would happen if you questioned a few of those facts, as they apply to your business or industry?

You could create a breakthrough that turns your market on its head, that's what.

To get started, try questioning of few of these "facts"...

- **"Fact:" Selling is hard!**
- **Questions**: What if selling were easy? How much more enthusiastically would you tell others about your business if you knew it would transform their lives? How would you go about selling if you KNEW prospects would buy?

- **"Fact:" My clients don't have money to spend these days!**
- **Questions**: What if you sold to wealthier clients? Or offered payment options? Or bundled services together to create a higher perceived value for the same price?

- **"Fact:" Nobody reads emails anymore!**
- **Questions**: Who said you had to rely on email only? What if you printed and mailed messages to prospects? Or faxed them? Or delivered them in person over coffee or in group seminars hosted by a joint-venture partner?

- **"Fact:" Client service is a cost I need to control!**
- **Questions**: What if client service were an investment in client *retention* or *referral generation* -- or both? What would you do differently? What would Zappos or Nordstrom do in your situation?

Bottom line: Many marketing "facts" are nothing more than assumptions. Why not question a few of them? It could lead you to breakthroughs that hit your market with the force of an atomic bomb.

Notes:

8) Get More Callbacks from Your Prospects

Has this ever happened to you?

A prospect sends an email or leaves a voicemail, inquiring about your services. You reply by email or phone and leave a message. You wait for them to call back. And wait ...

Stinks, doesn't it?

But ... what if you could get more people to return your voicemails or reply to your emails? You could make more sales, faster. And that would not stink.

After seeing sales expert Jill Konrath speak and reading her book, *SNAP Selling*, I made changes to my follow-up emails that paid off quickly -- a sales call with a prospect I had been chasing for days.

The solution from Konrath that worked so well is two words long: **pique curiosity**.

Normally, I can pique curiosity pretty well. You've read this far, haven't you?

But, for some reason, I couldn't get one particular prospect to schedule a call with me, following his initial inquiry about my copywriting services.

So, after reviewing pages 96-97 of Konrath's book, I sent the following email to Mr. Hard-to-Reach Prospect:

Thanks again for your inquiry yesterday; did you get my voicemail?

My schedule is full today, but if you have 20-30 minutes tomorrow, Wed., I can call between 3:00 and 4:30 pm ET to discuss your needs.

Please reply to let me know the best time/number for me to call you.

Also, Sam Smith said something on your LinkedIn profile that could be very helpful to you.

His email response came within the hour:

Wednesday @ 3:00 would be best.

Re-read the end of my email: *Also, Sam Smith said something on your LinkedIn profile that could be very helpful to you*.

His curiosity was piqued. And he scheduled a call with me to find out what the heck I was talking about. (Want to know what I found on his LinkedIn profile? Email me at k@clientcloningsystems.com and I'll tell you – if you're on LinkedIn, it's on your profile, too. And you're losing revenue every day that you don't fix it.)

As Konrath suggests in her book:

"After reviewing what you know about your targeted company and what's important to your prospective customer, determine what would pique their curiosity the most."

Do this: Send emails and leave voicemails that pique curiosity -- and watch your sales soar.

Because, as David Ogilvy once said, "You can't bore your customers into buying."

Notes:

9) Use the Client Reactivation Letter: Your Key to an Untapped Market

How's business?

Are you looking for new clients?

Question: Why spend 90% of your time beating the bushes, trying to convince total strangers to give you their money, when there's a rich, untapped market out there already?

This new market (as we learned in the Girl Scout example):

- knows you,
- trusts you,
- has the money to pay you, and
- wants you to succeed

This "new" market is ... your past clients.

Think about it. If you're any good at what you do and your personality isn't abusive, you should have no trouble re-selling to past clients.

And what's an easy way to re-sell to past clients? **A client reactivation letter**.

If you write and mail a good letter (email is a distant second best) to say, "I've missed you," "I want you back," and "Here's something special for you," it's fairly predictable that you will get a cash-flow surge in your business.

It's relatively easy to make a sale to past clients, because they've already trusted you enough to give you their money once.

And there's zero cost of acquisition, because you know where to find them.

As a copywriter, I write **lost client reactivation letters** for my clients all the time.

Here's an example below ...

Thank you!

Dear John,

November marks our 20th year in business -- and you made it possible!

When we started our company in 1990 we were really nervous ... excited ... unsure of our future. You welcomed us into your home, shared a few laughs and gave us the opportunity to fix your heat, air conditioning, appliances, etc. Your loyalty and words of gratitude have been essential to our success!

So we would like to thank you. As a token of our appreciation, you can take advantage of a special anniversary discount of $20.00 on your next service call. Just mention promo code "2020" when you call, and you'll get a better deal than anyone else.

Here's how my client, Kathleen, described the results she got with the **Client Reactivation Letter** above: *"You wrote our '20-year anniversary' sales letter of appreciation -- this resulted in 50+ service calls. Nothing could be finer!!!"*

How would you like 50+ phone calls from pre-sold, qualified prospects -- your past clients?

A good client reactivation letter can do that for you.

10) Sell More by Saying "Thank You!"

You know I'm a fan of mailing handwritten thank-you notes to clients. A. Big. Fan.

Thank-you notes pay big dividends, in my experience.

As William James wrote: "The deepest principle in human nature is the craving to be appreciated."

A thank-you note *mailed* to clients shows how much you appreciate them. You satisfy a craving when you do this. And your clients will always -- always -- reward you.

In his excellent book, *You, Inc.*, Harry Beckwith writes:

> "Handwritten thank-you notes feel like gifts because you took the time to find the paper and envelope, write the note, affix the stamp, and gift-wrap your note in its package."

Finally, to drive this point home, here are two mini-case studies from the book, *Thank You Power*, by Deborah Norville:

1. According to a 1995 study by Bruce Rind and Prashant Bordia, restaurant servers who wrote "Thank you" on the check before handing it to their customers **got tips averaging 11 percent more than servers who didn't** (emphasis mine).

The lesson here is simple: A simple, written "Thank you" can pay you back.

2. In another experiment, jewelry store customers were called to thank them for their business. Customers "spent more during return visits the following month than customers who didn't get a thank you call," writes Norville, continuing:

> But they also spent more than customers who got the thank you call and were told at the same time of an upcoming 20 percent-off sale. Word of the sale, which could be perceived as a pitch for more business, made the thank you ring hollow.

The lesson here is more complex: Your "Thank you" may hinder future sales *if* you do it wrong. While I've received -- and used -- discount coupons that came with thank-you notes, they may rub some people the wrong way, as in the jewelry store experiment.

So, as in all cases when you find a new marketing tactic, test it out.

Mail different combinations of thank-you notes, wording, etc., to your clients. Because you may be one thank-you note away from a major breakthrough. Testing will tell. But the only way to get it wrong is to mail no thank-you notes at all.

Seriously, what would an 11% jump in revenue mean for your business, like the restaurant servers enjoyed? You'll never know until you write to clients and say, "Thank you!"

11) Use the $400-Billion Secret that Built Google

What secret helped turn Google from a scrappy startup into one of the world's biggest companies, valued at $400 billion as of this writing?

It's simple. You can say it in one word: **Testing**.

After doing hundreds of marketing tests myself since 1996, I'm convinced that this secret to *unstoppable growth* has never been easier for "the little guy" to use.

Heck, Google will even let you use their testing tools for free. Don't worry, I will explain everything ...

But first, you may ask, what is testing?

Testing is simply pitting one version of a marketing piece against another, to see which gets more response, in the form of calls, inquiries, or sales.

You can test the headlines, prices, offers, guarantees, opening paragraphs in a sales letter, web pages, print ads, email blasts, or sales presentations.

As marketing blogger and author Dan Zarrella writes:

> No matter how well your ads, emails and landing pages are performing, they can always be doing better. That little bit of knowledge should eat away at any marketer or business owner worth her salt, and by not striving for constant improvement **you're leaving money on the table and letting your competition eat your lunch** (*bold in original*).

Testing is a <u>big</u> reason Google got so big, so fast.

You see, for years, Google has tested every key element on its web site. From the position of the search box, to the number of words on each page, Google has relentlessly optimized its search experience for users since going online in 1998.

Don't believe me? Here's one of the first known screenshots of Google, from **December 2, 1998**:

Less than 6 months later, on **April 23, 1999**, Google's home page looked like this:

And seven years later, on **December 2, 2005**, Google's home page looked like this:

Those changes were driven by users – customers. Versions of the web site that people clicked on were kept, and those that did not get clicks were discarded.

In a word, **testing** has been an essential to Google's growth. So pay careful attention here …

The most common type of testing is split testing or A/B testing. Here, you change <u>one</u> element in two marketing pieces that are otherwise identical, and expose them to the same audience.

Example: You test one ad with the headline "7 Days to a Flatter Stomach" and the other ad with the headline, "Lose Weight and Feel Great." One ad will almost always outperform the other, sometimes by as much as 80%, according to research.

The winning ad is called a "control." You then pit the control against another challenger and repeat the test to determine a new winner, testing only one element at a time.

Why not test multiple elements, like a new headline, a new price, a new guarantee, etc. – all at once?

Because when you change multiple elements, it's nearly impossible to pick out what exactly caused the change in response, unless you do multivariate testing -- but that's an advanced concept, beyond the scope of this guide.

So, test one thing at a time, until you have a clear winner.

If you're testing sales letters, you should mail at least 500 to 1,000 of each version to get a statistically valid result.

If you're testing web pages, good news: Google lets you use their testing software for free. I've used it for years and couldn't run my business without it. Want to try it?

It's called **Google Experiments**. To learn more, it's best to Google "Google Experiments" to find the web page that explains it, as the location sometimes changes.

OVERVIEW OF CONTENT EXPERIMENTS
Benefits of Experiments

<   NEXT: EXPERIMENTS REQUIREMENTS & SIGN-IN   >

If you have a website, you have activities that you want your visitors to complete
newsletter) and/or metrics that you want to improve (e.g., revenue, visit duration,
you can test which version of a landing page results in the greatest improvement

**Here's why testing is VITAL, whether it's done by
you or a copywriter who works for you**: Take a look
at the following result, from one of the hundreds of tests
I've run over the years ...

Free Audio CD Oct 26 2010
Paused - Resume | Stop | Follow Up | Copy | Settings | Report
Created: Oct 26, 2010 | Launched: Oct 26, 2010

☆ Combination 1 has a 99.4% chance of outperforming the original
Run a follow-up experiment to validate the results »

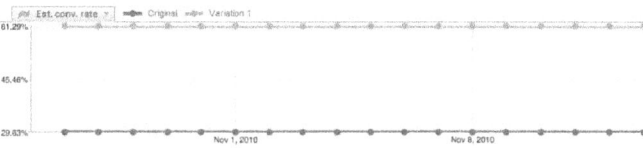

Variations (2)   Download: PDF XML CSV TSV | Print

Disable | All Combinations (2) ▼ | Key: ▦ Winner ░ Inconclusive ▉ Loser

Variation	Status	Est. conv. rate		Chance to Beat Orig.	Observed Improvement	Conv./Visitors
Original	Enabled	29.6% ± 12%		—	—	8 / 27

☆ Combination 1 has a 99.4% chance of outperforming the original. **Run a follow-up experiment »**

| Variation 1 | Enabled | 61.3% ± 12% | | 99.4% | 107% | 19 / 31 |

Show rows: 15 ▼   ⦀ ◄ 1 to 1 of 1 ► ⦀

See the two numbers above, circled in red -- 29.6% and
61.3%?

I pitted two versions of one web page against each other, designed to get people to sign up for a free audio CD. Both web pages were pretty good.

But one outperformed the other ... dramatically.

The **original web page** had a conversion rate of 29.6%, which is very good. It means that, for every 100 people who visit, about 29 "converted" and took the desired action.

In this case, I simply asked people to give me their name and email address. Upon doing so, Google counted them as a conversion.

In the **variation web page**, I made a few changes to the headline – and nothing more. The rest of the web page was identical to the original. But the results were not – 61.3% of visitors to that web page became leads. That's pretty incredible.

But that's not an increase of 31.7% (61.3% - 29.6%). No. It's much better than that. Look at the graphic again. The improvement in response was more than double -- 107%.

And lest you think that testing can take years and cost millions of dollars, let me tell you something: This breakthrough test took less than 14 days at a cost of $0.

Now ...

Imagine the best sales letter, web page, Yellow Pages ad, or print ad you ever used in your business. How much revenue did it bring in? Now ... double that number. That's the power of testing.

Are you leaving half your revenue and profits on the table?

Letting your competition eat your lunch?

Missing out on life-changing revenue that could banish your money worries for this year – and beyond?

You almost certainly are, if you're not testing.

As David Ogilvy said, "Never stop testing, and your advertising will never stop improving."

Notes:

12) Make Service Your Ultimate Weapon

Want to see a customer service manual that's worth $1.2 billion and is updated every day? Just plug "Zappos review" into Google, read, and emulate.

Example: Here's one review that I found recently ...

⭐⭐⭐⭐⭐ **5/5**   ⓘ posted Sep-06-2013

"Incredible. On all accounts. There is no complaint even possible. Nothing for me to be even slightly dissatisfied. I bought a pair of Vans Core Classics from Zappos. Within the first few weeks, they started falling apart. The vulcanized sole started to separate from the lower of the shoe. The rubber also split. I decided to just keep wearing them. 4 months later, I noticed that the split rubber had chafed against the lower and worn a hole in the shoe.

I contacted Zappos with a very low pressure email, just informing them of the poor quality shoes and with a polite request to give me a price break on some new shoes. Shot in the dark right? They're 4 month old daily worn shoes, what can I reasonably expect? I told them that if they couldn't do anything for me, I would completely understand and I would still buy from them. I expected them to throw me a bone...maybe 10% off or something. Nope. They sent an awesomely detailed, apologetic, and humorous email within half an hour. They credited me my ENTIRE purchase price towards a new pair of shoes of my choice, and they requested no pictures of the shoes nor did they require a return. They told me to donate the shoes or use them as an art project. :) They also added me to the VIP program, which offers free one day shipping.

This is the way to do customer service. As a "thank you" I bought another pair of shoes from them (at full cost) that I wouldn't have bought otherwise.

Your takeaway: You canNOT buy or create advertising any better than the testimonial above. When you deliver outrageous service that not only delights but delightfully surprises your clients, you've got a recipe for explosive growth.

Good news: You don't have to delight your clients with what you actually sell to delight your clients.

Read that sentence again. I'll wait.

You see, Zappos sells shoes. But the 5-star raving testimonial above (one of thousands like it you can find online) is not about shoes. It's about the delightful surprise this customer experienced when receiving a rapid, hassle-free refund.

And before you gripe about refunds, know that this one resulted in:
1. valuable free publicity (here and elsewhere)
2. a second purchase at full price
3. a customer for life

Any business can do that. Including yours. So, the only thing stopping you from delivering the same kind of billion-dollar service as Zappos is ... you.

And, yes, the way Zappos treats customers is worth $1.2 billion. Because it was legendary service like the example above that made Zappos worth the $1.2 billion that Amazon paid for it in 2009.

Notes:

13) Use 80/20 Thinking for More Profits

There's a limited number of hours in every day -- 24, to be exact.

That means there isn't time to do everything. There are some things you can't do ... and more things you shouldn't do.

Especially when it comes to your clients.

The less time you waste serving the wrong clients -- people who complain about price, are slow to pay, don't appreciate what you do, etc. -- the more time you can invest serving the right clients -- those people who cheerfully pay your fees, appreciate what you do, and refer others like them.

So, stop talking to any more of the wrong clients and start talking to more of the right clients.

How can you tell who is who? By doing "80/20 Thinking."

In the book, *The 80/20 Principle: The Secret to Achieving More with Less,* Richard Koch writes:

> *To engage in 80/20 Thinking, we must constantly ask ourselves: what is the 20 percent that is leading to 80 percent? What are the vital few inputs or causes, as opposed to the trivial many? Where is the haunting melody being drowned out by the background noise?*

When you engage in 80/20 Thinking, you find that a large percentage of revenue comes from a small percentage of clients.

Implication? Spend more time with those precious few clients! Examples:

- 85% of your revenue comes from clients who live within 20 miles of your business.
- 62% of your revenue comes from 3 client segments: repair shops, bookkeepers, and trainers.
- 78% of your revenue comes from clients who belong to the Chamber of Commerce.

Important: The actual amount will rarely be 80%, but it *will* be disproportionately large. Look for any big output coming from a small input.

When I applied 80/20 Thinking to my resume writing service back in 1999, I found that about 70% of revenue came from 4 kinds of clients: sales, marketing, IT, and management professionals.

I liked doing business with those clients. They were smart, didn't complain about price, and got good results from my service, which led them to refer others.

So guess what? I added a line to my Yellow Pages ad to attract more clients like them. It read as follows: "Specializing in resumes for sales, marketing, IT, and management professionals."

A little thing, right? But it had a <u>big</u> impact. I started getting calls from more of my idea clients -- sales, marketing, IT, and management professionals. Because I had flagged them with my ad.

You can do this, too, and get more clients like your best clients. But not until you first identify which clients *are* your best clients.

Now, don't forget -- there's a flip side to clients you love. This would be clients you ... don't love.

Example: If you find 72% of your problems come from orthodontists and social workers and you HATE working with orthodontists and social workers, STOP working with them.

When I identified the 20% of clients who gave me 80% of my problems, I created an "undesirable" status for them in my Goldmine database. Those people (from certain industries that shall remain nameless) never heard from me again. And if they tried to re-hire me for a project, I politely declined.

Does this sound cold? Odd? Weird?

Consider: No matter how well you serve people, a certain number will *never* be happy, no matter what.

Then consider: Time isn't money. Time is everything. Time is all we have each day. So ... do <u>not</u> waste your precious time on people you don't enjoy serving.

80/20 Thinking eliminated nearly all my client service headaches in a few weeks, while attracting more ideal clients. My business grew and I had more fun.

80/20 Thinking can work wonders for your client service and your business, too. Try it.

Notes:

14) Fix Complaints for a 95% Return on Investment

Fact: Clients who complain are more interested in working with you than clients who say nothing.

Think about it. If you get awful service from a vendor you will never use again, you likely won't go back to complain. Instead, you will simply take your business elsewhere.

So do whatever it takes to "save" complaining clients. Do it because these people secretly want to keep working with you. And because the payoffs can be huge ...

I remember Sharon, a client of my resume service back in 1998. Upon seeing the first draft of my work for her, she said, "Oh, this has problems. I don't like this."

My reply: "Thanks for letting me know that. Please tell me everything that's bothering you and why."

We then went through her resume, line by line. In the end, she was delighted with the result. And she later referred more than 8 new clients and several thousand dollars in revenue to my business.

That's just one example.

According to an article by Lindsay Willott on the web site, www.CustomerThermometer.com:

Fixing problems turns angry customers into loyal advocates. Jake Poore, who looked after "service recovery" for Disney says "everyone makes mistakes, that's human.

But how do you solicit those mistakes and rectify them so that the story is now possibly better than if there were no mistake at all?"

He makes the point that customers who go home mad tell their story, whereas those who go home happy tell your story. Often a bad experience that was turned around makes for a happier customer and a better story than a customer who had a good experience in the first place.

Below is a graphic to show the **loyalty** that develops over time, after you fix a problem to your customer's satisfaction ...

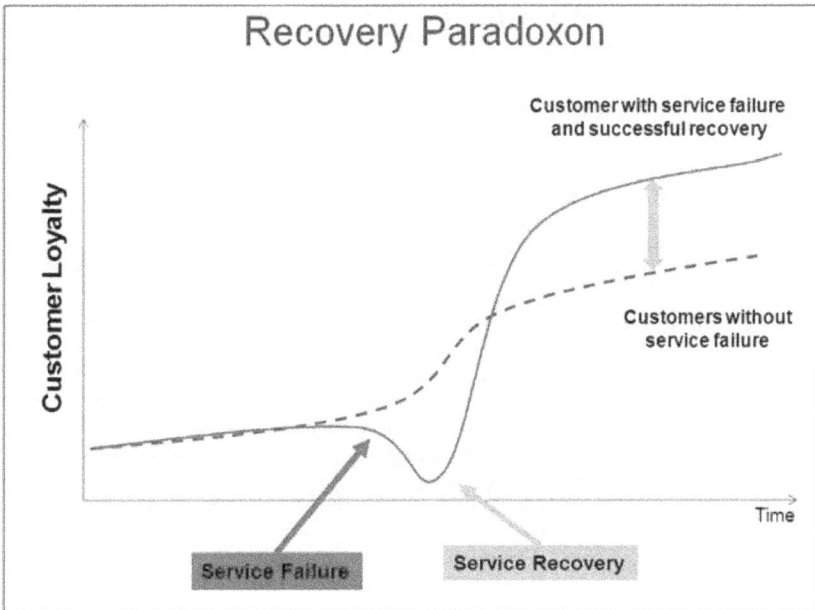

Recovery Paradoxon

Customer Loyalty / Time

Customer with service failure and successful recovery

Customers without service failure

Service Failure

Service Recovery

(Used by kind permission of CustomerThermometer.com)

According to "Manage Complaints to Enhance Loyalty," an article by John Goodman in the Feb. 2006 issue of *Quality Progress*, **solving customer complaints pays you back with a 95% profit for the time and effort invested**:

The following are cost-benefit calculations for getting customers to complain and satisfying them. The assumptions are:

- A customer is worth at least $30 in profit over a year's time.
- The cost of handling a complaint is about $5.
- At least 75% of callers are satisfied.
- To quantify the payoff of soliciting and handling complaints, it's critical to know the rate of the prevalence of noncomplainants and their loyalty as well as the loyalty of those who complain and are not satisfied.

The calculation for moving a customer with a problem from noncomplainant to satisfied complainant follows:

- Payoff due to improved loyalty. Typically, moving a customer with a problem from noncomplainant to complainant to a satisfied caller raises loyalty by about 30%, meaning, conservatively, handling a customer at a cost of $5 will give you a payoff of (.30 increase in loyalty) x (.75 satisfied) x $30 value = $6.75.

After covering the $5 cost of handling the complaint, you are left with $1.75 profit and or an ROI of 35% ($1.75/$5 cost to handle)

Goodman goes on to detail the total return-on-investment of 95% from the increased referrals that come from fixing complaints:

If, conservatively, one out of 10 satisfied customers produces a word-of-mouth referral and one new customer worth $30 is won for every 40 who hear good things, then satisfying 10 customers adds $30 in word-of-mouth benefits, or $3 for each customer satisfied (10 customers satisfied times four positive referrals per satisfied customer times one new customer for each 40 hearing positive referrals).

That adds an additional $3 payoff for each customer satisfied, raising the ROI to 95% ($1.75 + $3.00)/$5.00. The preceding calculation is a simple estimate of the impact of positive word of mouth produced by good service on loyalty and profits.

And consider this: Southwest Airlines hired a *Chief Apology Officer*, who "spends his 12-hour work days finding out how Southwest disappointed its customers and then firing off homespun letters of apology," according to a March 18, 2007 article by Jeff Bailey in The New York Times.

Which explains why Southwest Airlines may be the only airline in America with actual fans.

Bottom Line: Do whatever it takes to satisfy complaining clients. See every service problem as a chance for you to triumph. When you do, your happy clients will tell their friends.

A customer service "recovery" can be as valuable as delivering good service the first time. So, never run from complaints. Instead, rush to solve them. Then encourage your clients to share their happiness with others.

Notes:

15) Discover the 39,900% ROI of a Simple "Thank You"

A client tipped me off to a story on Minnesota Public Radio about a "new" marketing strategy to build your business.

First, read this interview with a small business owner ...

> **Brett Brohl:** I've written, at least 2,000 thank yous just in the last 12 months.
>
> Brett Brohl owns Scrubadoo.com. He sells medical scrubs. You know, those pastel-colored outfits, doctors and nurses wear. Brohl says he hand writes a thank you note for every single customer. Scrubadoo is a new company, and Brohl says there are a lot of websites out there selling the exact same products he does.
>
> **Brett Brohl:** If you Google the word "scrubs," we're not on the front page, we're not on the second page. And just like every other industry right now, competition's tough and with less people buying, it's even tougher.
>
> Brohl says, a new company like his can't afford major marketing like TV commercials. Instead, he says, he's counting on thank you notes to help Scrubadoo stand out.

Heh. Did you get that?

Google may rank your competitors higher than you, but one thing Google can't control is *the personal touch*. You can give out as much of that as you'd like. One way to do that is to send a personal touch by mail, in the form of a thank-you note. For the price of a stamp, you get 100% of that person's attention.

You may know that I write regularly about the power of "thank you" in business. And with good reason.

While writing and mailing thank-you notes is "no-tech" and slower than email, the ROI can be incredible. When I say incredible, how does a 39,900% ROI sound?

How? Read on ...

> Sarah Siewert is 24, she lives in Chicago. A couple of months ago, she hit up a department store with her mom and her sister. They were shopping for purses.
>
> **Sarah Siewert:** And as soon as we got there, into the purse section, one of the saleswomen immediately approached us and was really attentive, she pulled purses from the back, she went through different options, different colors
>
> Typical shopping experience, right? As long as you get an attentive sales person, like Sarah did. She and her mom ended up buying a purse apiece. Then, a couple weeks later they both got letters in the mail from the saleswoman who'd helped them. They were thank you notes.
>
> **Siewert:** It was a fully hand written note, referencing the exact bag we purchased. And on my note, she even had a nice reference to our alma mater.
>
> Turns out they'd gone to the same school. And, I'll admit the purse Sarah bought wasn't exactly

cheap. It was Marc Jacobs, about $400. [And] it worked. Siewert says she just bought another bag.

Let's do the math.

After getting a thank-you note in the mail, which cost about $1 to send -- including postage -- Siewert returned to buy another purse. If she spent another $400 on a similar bag, that's a return on investment of 39,900%.

Thank me later. Right now, you've got some thank-you notes to mail.

Notes:

16) How to Serve Clients Better and Get More Revenue

Want to make more money in your business, starting today? Offer an upsell.

Simply create a deluxe version of whatever you sell -- raise the price 20-50% and add a higher level of service. When you do, about 20% or more of your clients will choose the higher-price option.

How can you offer more service to justify a higher price?

- **Deliver faster** -- offer "emergency" rates for same-day or priority service; ship FedEx Priority Overnight instead of U.S. Mail
- **Deliver more** -- add 20-50% of whatever it is you deliver, like super-sizing an order of French fries
- **Deliver better** -- offer 2-3 Special Reports or a Quick Start Guide to help clients get better results

In nearly 20 years of marketing, I have never seen an upsell fail to add more profits to the bottom line. Because, at least 20% of your clients will almost always choose the higher-price option.

The only real obstacle to this is in your head: You probably think your business is "different," your clients can't afford it, or they don't really need a deluxe version.

News Flash: You are not your clients.

The surest way to under-serve your market and leave money on the table is to have contempt for a new marketing idea like this prior to investigating it for yourself.

Don't be contemptuous of new ideas. Try them. Starting with this one: Offer an upsell.

Notes:

17) Stop Selling a Service. Start Selling This

"If you're selling a service, you're selling a relationship," writes Harry Beckwith in the excellent book, *Selling the Invisible: A Field Guide to Modern Marketing*. He adds:

> Most companies in expert services -- such as lawyers, doctors, and accountants -- think that their clients are buying expertise. But most prospects for these complex services cannot evaluate expertise; they cannot tell a really good tax return, a clever motion, or a perceptive diagnosis. But they can tell if the relationship is good and if phone calls are returned. Clients are experts a knowing if they feel valued.

> In most professional services, you are not really selling expertise -- because your expertise is assumed .... Instead, you are selling a relationship. And in most cases, that is where you need the most work.

How can you better sell the unique and valuable relationship that clients will get by doing business with you?

Try these ideas:

- **Change your voicemail greeting** to something warm and personal, instead of cold and corporate. Here's mine:

  "Hi this is Kevin Donlin at Client Cloning Systems. If you are Governor Dayton calling me back -- or want to get a return on investment of at least

300% on the sales copy I write for you -- please leave your callback information at the tone. I'm probably IN the office, because I am a workaholic, and if it's not Saturday or Sunday -- or midnight -- I will call you back today. Thank you!"

- **Return all phone calls within 90 minutes ... and say so on your voicemail greeting**. (I did this for years and won at least one new client *every year* from someone who timed my callback and was suitably impressed.)

- **Learn one interesting, personal fact about your prospect and bring it up on your next call**. The answers are out here. I always try to remark about a person's college degree, hobbies, associations or other data on their LinkedIn profiles. It breaks the ice -- every time.

- **Make your intangible service tangible** ... by meeting for coffee this week, mailing a thank-you note, or introducing your client to a prospect (or vice-versa).

Notes:

18) Hit the "Target 25"

I interviewed speaker and author Mark LeBlanc about his "Target 25" strategy -- talking on a regular basis to 25 people who can make a difference in your business. This is *good stuff* ...

Kevin: What is the Target 25, exactly?

Mark: It is my advocate strategy. Every one of us has a group of people who believe in us and our work. I call them our advocates. A couple of other terms are cheerleaders and champions. Who believes in you and your work?

In the Target 25 Strategy, you identify the 25 advocates in your life and work who are in a position to impact your business, and then you make a connection with them every 30 days. Not to ask them for referrals but just simply to create "top of mind presence."

If these are the people who believe in you and your work and are most likely to go out of their way, or make a positive connection, or open a door on your behalf, they're more likely to do it with "top of mind presence." Time goes by so fast that all of a sudden 10 months or three years have passed and you think, "Where are those people who used to give me referrals?"

Kevin: That's a great idea because more contacts lead to more sales. It may not be today that I refer someone to you but in three months, bam! I may hit you on the right day. It can't happen if you're waiting for the phone to ring. It has to be proactive and systematic.

Now, you mentioned that 25 is a good number of contacts. Why isn't 50 better, or 100 best? Why limit it to 25?

Mark: I think once you start going beyond 25, it gets harder to manage these people on a regular basis, and then it just becomes diluted with what I call "supporters."

I'm very blessed to have hundreds of supporters in my work but that group of advocates is a little bit smaller, and I would rather stay connected with them every 30 days.

Now, the sort of graduate school level of the advocate strategy is that you begin to put together a different advocate group if you have different profit centers.

For example, I have a coaching Target 25 group, and I also have a speaking Target 25 group of advocates. They're two different groups of advocates that refer me or believe in me for different ways in which I deliver my work.

Kevin: Thanks, Mark. This is an excellent way to stay connected with the people who can help us most. Those monthly contacts can include meeting for coffee, an article by email, a phone call, an introduction, etc. The important thing is to try this concept today!

Resource: Learn more about Mark at www.MarkLeBlanc.com

19) Learn How to Make $1.92 Million an Hour

Just over 12 months ago, I met a very influential person in the field of marketing -- a "guru to the gurus" type of guy. We'll call him, Jim.

Jim had just given a speech at a conference I attended last year. The room went wild. We all loved his talk.

Afterwards, during the break, I sprinted across the lobby to hop on an elevator to go up to my room. There was one other person in the elevator -- Jim.

As the door closed, I had about 30 seconds to give a *literal* elevator pitch before we both reached our floors.

But I didn't spew out some memorized spiel about how great I was or how we should do business together.

Instead, I simply told him that I loved his talk, told him why, and then asked him a reasonably intelligent question about marketing. He replied, and we struck up a nice conversation that continued after we reached our floor. I think we spoke for 2 minutes total.

Jim agreed to chat with me later at the conference, which we did.

Then, a few weeks later, Jim referred a dream client to me. I did good work and the client was delighted.

Then, Jim referred another client. And another. And another.

To date, Jim has sent me more than $64,000 in revenue -- and counting. In just a few short months, he's opened doors to people and projects that might have taken me years to find on my own.

And it all started with a 2-minute conversation.

When you do the math, the $64,000 in referrals I earned from those 2 minutes works out to $1,920,000 per hour.

Could I reasonably expect to earn that kind of money per hour again? And could you?

The answer to both questions is yes. Here's how ...

- If you went on TV and gave a 2-minute pitch for your business to the right audience, at the right time of day, you could easily top $1.92 million in revenue.
- Or if you spoke for an hour to a roomful of 1,000 prospects and convinced just 150 of them to pay you $12,800 (very doable), you could earn $1.92 million.
- Etc. etc.

While I hope you get a chance to deliver such a pitch on TV or to 1,000 prospects, this isn't about advertising on TV or seminar selling.

This is about another idea: Little actions can have BIG results.

Every person who calls you ... every email you get ... every chance encounter at a conference -- they all have the power to deliver life-changing revenue for your business.

That's the good news.

The bad news? If you're sitting in a seminar updating Twitter on your smartphone, or you're mentally checked out because you're having a bad day ... you can easily miss those $1,920,000-an-hour opportunities. Buecase they often come disguised as ordinary conversations -- not shiny golden tickets.

So, little actions can have BIG results. And they're more likely to pay off if your eyes are open and your mind is engaged.

Tip: Take 30 minutes this week, look through your database, and find the source of all your clients for the year to date. I predict you will be shocked at what you find -- good and bad.

You might even find you got $64,000 in revenue (or more) from a single, chance encounter, as I did. But you'll never know until you run the numbers and see.

Why not take a look right now? You'll be glad you did.

Notes:

20) Get More Sales Tomorrow by Doing This Today

Here's a simple idea that can make you a lot of money for your business, starting tomorrow.

It's this: **Offer a money-back guarantee.**

Because, if you make it risk-free to buy from you ... more people will buy from you.

Few businesses truly guarantee what they sell. So the opportunity for you to stand out in your industry is staggering.

Before going any further, here's a quick quiz ...

Look at the following list of successful companies. What one thing do they have in common?

- Zappos
- Amazon
- Nordstrom
- FedEx

Answer: Each rose to the top of their industry using strong guarantees of satisfaction. By strong, I mean offering to refund the purchase price or easily exchange the item.

These companies reversed the risk of doing business. Customers got another reason to buy today, without fear of looking bad tomorrow. And tremendous profits followed.

Guarantees are not new, of course.

They've been used by successful mail-order companies for decades. Companies like L.L. Bean, The Teaching Company, and SkyMall, to name a few.

They're hugely successful today, yet they were once small businesses. Perhaps smaller than yours. But their sales surged after customers knew they could buy without fear of being stuck with an item they didn't like.

Yet ... guarantees *horrify* many small business owners.

If you're like most, it might only take five or six big refunds in a month to spell financial trouble.

Yet, the way I see it, you shouldn't worry. Because you already have a guarantee -- you just don't know it. Let me explain ...

If a customer called to complain about the work you did, what would you do? Offer to redo or replace it, probably. Because it's a smart investment of your time and money to satisfy one current customer now than it is to combat a lot of bad word-of-mouth later.

Especially when you consider that, according to one study, a satisfied customer will tell one or two others about your company. But an unsatisfied customer will tell 9 people -- or more. You need to put those numbers in your favor. You need to satisfy your customers. And a guarantee makes it all possible.

There's more.

In my experience since 1996, only about 2-5% of customers will ever ask for their money back if offered a refund, no matter what you're selling -- as long as your quality and service are good.

So, guarantees are more of a safe bet than a calculated risk.

Now. How specific and outrageous of a guarantee can you think of? What guarantee would set your industry on its ear? What would keep your competitors up all night throwing darts at your picture?

That's the guarantee you want.

Yes, you will eventually give refunds. But if your sales increase 25%, 50%, 100% -- will you really care?

Here are example guarantees to get your mind in gear. Which one would be easiest for you to modify and use?

- Real estate agent: I'll sell your home in 90 days. Or you get $1,000 cash.
- Restaurant: You'll love our food. Or your next meal is free.
- Sports therapist: We'll stop your pain in 24 hours. Or your money back.
- Dog walking service: We'll be there on time, every time. Or you get a $50 bag of dog food -- Free.
- Florist: Guaranteed "gasp" when she gets our flowers. Or she gets a free box of chocolates.

But wait. There are two ways you can screw up a guarantee ...

1) Fail to put teeth in your guarantee.
There must be a penalty if you fail to deliver. So, if you say "Satisfaction guaranteed" ... and nothing else, you're not saying anything. And your sales will stay flat as a result.

2) Fail to perform on a massive scale.
Example: if British Petroleum had guaranteed "spill-free" oil wells, that might have produced an even bigger, more-expensive PR nightmare for them in 2010.

To avoid failure on a massive scale, test on a small scale. This is vital. You must know how well your guarantee is performing before you roll it out to the whole world.

How to test?

You might advertise the guarantee on a special Web page, visible only to people who come there after reading a special promotion or Google AdWords ad. Or mention it on your voicemail message. Or on one set of business cards. Or in a letter you mail to one segment of your customer base.

You could test 45-, 60-, 90-, or 365-day money-back guarantees, for example. (Longer guarantees almost always work better.) You might even use a lifetime guarantee. Experiment!

You can devise a guarantee based on how fast you fill orders, how fast you deliver them, whether you'll always have a certain item in stock, etc.

Done right -- by testing on a small scale -- a guarantee can remove the risk of doing business with you. As a result, you can get more clients like your best clients, without advertising any more than you do now.

Notes:

21) Five Final Questions

Question 1: How much of your revenue comes from current clients?

Is it 50%? 80%? Wrong.

<u>100% of revenue comes from current clients</u>. Because the only people who can give you revenue are the people who buy from you. Prospects don't pay you -- they haven't bought anything yet.

Question 2: How much is your **marketing budget** -- the money you spend to chase after strangers, i.e., prospects?

Question 3: How much is your **client retention budget** -- the money you invest to make sure that the people who buy from you ... keep buying from you?

Question 4: Why is your client retention budget so much smaller than your marketing budget?

Question 5: What are you going to do about this?

About the Author

Kevin Donlin is a **marketing strategist**, **copywriter**, **author** and **speaker** in the Minneapolis area. Kevin:

... has been marketing since 1994, when he may have sold the first ebook online, "How to Find a Job on the Internet" (for $10, payable by check)

...was Webmaster for FedEx.com from 1995 (when the site had 6 web pages) until 1998 (*more* web pages)

... has been interviewed on marketing-related topics by Fox News, ABC-TV, NBC-TV, CBS Radio, *The Wall Street Journal*, *The New York Times*, *Fortune*, *Entrepreneur*, and many others

Kevin Donlin, interviewed on marketing strategy by Fox News

... was featured by Dan Kennedy in his book, *No BS Branding*, with two of his ads (on pages 119 and 120)

Clients hire Kevin to generate leads and sales for them by writing **direct mail, email promotions, web pages,** and **print ads.**

On a personal note, Kevin:

- has held jobs as a cashier, dishwasher, factory laborer, guitar player, landscaper, marketing copywriter, paper boy, record store manager, resume writer, stock boy, teacher, textbook writer, warehouse worker, and webmaster, among others (so he can understand nearly any business, including *yours*) ...

- has studied German, Greek, Irish, Japanese, Latin, Russian, and Spanish (so he can speak the language of almost anyone you want to sell to) ...

- lived and worked in Japan for 2.5 years, where the customer is not king -- the customer is <u>God</u> (so you work with a pro who "gets" client service, not some temperamental flake) ...

- has 1.95 college degrees, including a B.A. from Michigan State University, where he was a National Merit Scholar (so you benefit from his love of learning, which keeps him up-to-date on marketing tactics) ...

- believes fervently that entrepreneurs are the <u>last</u>, <u>best</u> hope for taking back America.

The End?

That's the end of this book. But I hope it's only the beginning for you ...

The beginning of more sales, profits, and peace of mind in your business. Can I help you get there faster? Maybe. But I'm not for everyone ...

The clients I work with best are presidents and CEOs of successful businesses (because I can't multiply zeroes) ... you're doing $1 million to $20 million in revenue ... you <u>must</u> understand and be a fan of direct-response marketing ... you must use direct mail (or be eager to try it) ... and you must be open to new ideas.

I specialize in the following:
1. **Client Reactivation campaigns** (new sales from old clients)
2. **Lead Generation campaigns** (hot new prospects via direct mail or online)
3. **Shock and Awe packages** (if you don't know what this means, just ask!)
4. **Increased Conversions** (improving your current sales and marketing process)

Still interested? If so, I might be able to do for you what I've done for them ...

$193,000 in new revenues from old clients!

"Within 24 hours ... I put the principles into practice by making some calls to existing clients for my company. One call netted a sale for $193,000 ... not a bad way to start the day. This stuff works!"

- David Bullock, Fanuc Robotics; Murfreesboro, TN

$77,098 in new revenues from old clients!

"We mailed the letter Kevin wrote. It was our first time to send a direct-mail promotion like this to existing accounts already on the books. The results were pretty incredible -- $77,098 in new revenues, with more to come by the end of the year. The return on investment for your services was off the charts!"

- Jeff Prouty, Chairman and Founder,
the Prouty Project; Eden Prairie, MN

$32,400 in new revenue from "dead" email list!

"In our initial email, we had a total of 30 phone calls and email requests for assistance from 2,291 emails sent. Far better response than we ever had before. In recent years, lucky to get 3 to 5 responses. We sold $32,400 in travel packages, including a trip to Tahiti and a Jamaica honeymoon. Great work!"

- Earl Milbrath, President, Travel Advisors Int.;
Chanhassen, MN

Beat expectations by nearly 400%!

"Your first letter performed outstanding! We got $2.41 in revenue for every name mailed. Craig said he would have been happy with 50 cents. Nice start. I guess you don't have to refund your fee now!"

- Steve Adams, President, Pets Supplies PLUS;
Muskegon, MI

Got 3 accounts with Wal-Mart and couldn't handle any more work!

"We had very good results from the direct marketing letter Kevin Donlin wrote for my commercial cleaning company. I got one large account with a mall and 3 additional accounts with Wal-Mart. I had to stop mailing letters because I can't handle any more work -- a nice problem to have. I thank you for that."

- Rob MacDougall, President, Crown Property Maint.; Urbandale, IA

$250,000 in the pipeline in 7 days!

"After we started testing the sales letter that you worked on for us, the phone started to ring, people started to call, and it started to work automatically. Seven days ago, I got an offer accepted from a guy -- I did no negotiating with him -- he got your package in the mail, he called and said yes. I'm going to make $115,000 on that deal. In the last 7 days, I've got $250,000 lined up as a result of the work we've done with you. I couldn't be happier with the work that you've done for us, Kevin. It's money well spent."

- Ryan Skalla, Real Estate Investment Properties; Corona, CA

Kevin is simply the best!

"We send clients to Kevin Donlin on a regular basis because he has a proven track record of success. He recently wrote a piece for one of our clients that returned $2.41 in profit for every name mailed! Kevin is simply the best. We love the fact that when we refer a client to him, they come back RAVING about his work."

- Craig Simpson, President, Simpson Direct; Grants Pass, OR

300% better response and 3:1 payback!

"Kevin has done a great job for us. The postcards have been very successful. We are generating 4 times the response we were able to generate on our own and the payback is about 3:1. In fact, we are so happy with the results that we are developing new direct-mail campaigns with Kevin to further leverage this. He is very responsive, deadline driven, and actually listens to our needs. We are very satisfied with our return on investment."

- Joshua Haberman and Todd Bacon, Alexander & Haberman Insurance; St. Paul, MN

Thousands of dollars in extra sales!

"Kevin's simple techniques have helped me gain thousands of dollars in additional sales automatically. Example: he showed me how to use email in a way that produced more than $4,000 in new revenue by creating a system in 1-2 hours that runs forever."

- Dan Janal, Founder, PRLeads.com; Excelsior, MN

Kevin did a campaign that was perfect!

"Kevin 'gets it!' I only had to explain what I needed to do one time and he was back quickly with a campaign that was perfect for us. His efforts were indispensable in rolling out a new product to the right market in a timely manner."

- Terry Slattery, CEO, Slattery Sales Group; Edina, MN

Kevin knows how to generate profits!

"Kevin knows how to market and generate profits! As a successful business owner myself for more than 10 years, I thought I knew everything I needed to know about profitable growth. But every time I listen to Kevin, I come away with at least one new strategy or tactic that puts money in my bank account -- more often than not, a lot of money. If you're looking to increase your revenues and profits, I strongly recommend listening to Kevin."

- Steven Rothberg, President and Founder, CollegeRecruiter.com

Increased revenue nearly 700% with a marketing machine!

"Before working with Kevin, I was getting new clients from the newspaper at a net of about $12 each. But using the ad Kevin wrote for my insurance agency, I got 6 new clients from one small-town newspaper at a net of $92.50 each on their first purchase, with a great chance to sell them additional services later. Kevin's ads are a marketing machine I can depend on."

- Greg Young, Greg Young Insurance Agency; Hugo, MN

Still reading? Great. If you qualify and if you think I'm talking to you, let's take the next step together ...

As a buyer of this book, you're entitled to a Free Marketing Strategy Session by phone and a Free Surprise Gift.

Please note: I do NOT give out free sessions willy nilly, because my time bills at more than $500 an hour. But because you're a book buyer (and, more importantly, a book *reader*), you will almost certainly benefit from the ideas we'll exchange by phone. So I'd love to speak with you very soon!

Visit www.ClientCloningSystems.com to learn more and contact me.

Or, send an email to k@ClientCloningSystems.com and I'll reply within one business day with details about your Free Marketing Strategy Session and Free Surprise Gift (while supplies last).

Kevin Donlin
Marketing Strategist + Copywriter + Author

Offer subject to change without notice